God's LIFE in YOU

OSBORN
Ministries
International

USA HQ:

OSBORN MINISTRIES, INT'L

P.O. Box 10, Tulsa, OK 74102 USA

T.L. & DAISY OSBORN, CO-FOUNDERS
LADONNA C. OSBORN, CEO

Tel: 918/743-6231
Fax: 918/749-0339
E-Mail: ministry@osborn.org
www.osborn.org

Canada: Box 281 STN ADELAIDE, Toronto ON M5C 2J4
England: Box 148, Birmingham B3 2LG
(A Registered Charity)

BIBLE QUOTATIONS IN THIS BOOK MAY
BE PERSONALIZED, PARAPHRASED, ABRIDGED OR
CONFORMED TO THE *PERSON* AND *TENSE* OF THEIR
CONTEXT IN ORDER TO FOSTER CLARITY AND
INDIVIDUAL APPLICATION. VARIOUS LANGUAGE
TRANSLATIONS AND VERSIONS HAVE BEEN CON-
SIDERED. BIBLICAL REFERENCES ENABLE THE
READER TO COMPARE THE PASSAGES WITH HIS OR
HER OWN BIBLE.

THE AUTHOR

ISBN 978-0-87943-191-4
Copyright 2012 by LaDonna C. Osborn
Printed in USA 2012-09
All Rights Reserved

CONTENTS

DEDICATED

This book is dedicated to people in every nation who deserve to know and fully understand the greatness of the life of Christ at work in them—when they believe on Him and accept Him as their personal Savior and Lord.

—T.L. Osborn

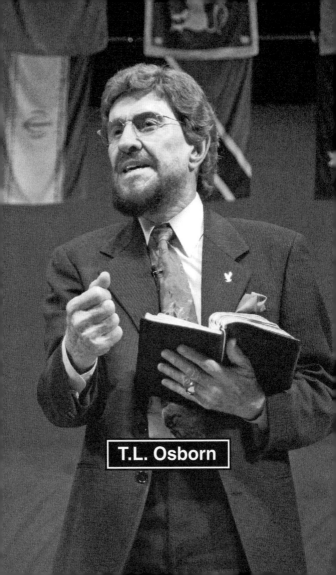
T.L. Osborn

Introduction

FOR OVER 60 years my father has presented to the world, in written form, the most essential and energizing biblical truths that produce the Christ-life in people.

This book, GOD'S LIFE IN YOU, will become a favorite and reliable resource as you continue to discover what it means to be a carrier of God's life. Study and embrace the 52 facts that are included herein, which establish your faith in the fundamental and unchanging truths that are for you.

If you have received Jesus Christ as your personal Savior, then you no longer need grovel or beg for forgiveness of sin or for the dignity that comes to you through Christ. Likewise, you are not required to continually fight the devil or struggle to live a life of peace and purpose.

It is GOD'S LIFE IN YOU that makes the difference. Know these truths. Embrace and believe each one. Determine to LIVE each day according to the redemptive reality of GOD'S LIFE IN YOU.

LaDonna C. Osborn, D.Min.

Chapter 1

–Discover–
God's Purpose in You

WHEN YOU DISCOVER your roots in God and identify with His purpose for you on this earth, you have begun to really live **GOD'S LIFE IN YOU**.

It is a lifestyle based on:

- Positive *faith,*

- Positive *thinking,*

- Positive *talking,*

- Positive *acting.*

What is the source of this positive faith?

> *Faith comes by hearing the word of God.* Rom.10:17

Here are *fifty-two facts* which lift you from boring mediocrity to a fruitful partnership with God. They are the miracle stepping stones that lead you from the condemning guilt-complex of living out of harmony and out of contact with God to the success and exhilarating self-esteem which develops when you discover who you are and how you can come to God and share His lifestyle.

You discover a *new power*, a *new goal* and *new purpose*.

You are transformed:

> From defeat — To success
>
> From sickness — To health
>
> From boredom — To enthusiasm
>
> From problems — To solutions

From pressure — To pleasure

From poverty — To prosperity

From hopelessness — To happiness

You are blessed, and your family is benefited too.

The Bible says: *Old things are passed away; behold, all things are become new.*[2Cor.5:17]

These *fifty-two facts* will help you to experience GOD'S LIFE IN YOU. Then they become the foundation stones of God's pact of plenty — His full life policy that covers you and your house.

- Review them often.

- Rehearse them in prayer.

- Memorize them.

- Recite them in family worship.

- Recount them to relatives and to friends.

- Enumerate them.

They will continually activate GOD'S LIFE IN YOU as you keep them in your heart and on your lips.

Anyone who embarks on this good life will, sooner or later, discover a very real enemy. The Bible calls him Satan and mentions him at least 175 times by such names as *Lucifer*,[Isa.14:12-14] *the devil*,[Mat.4:1; Eph. 6:11] and *Satan*,[Rev.12:9] *the adversary*,[1Pet.5:8] *the god of this world*,[2Cor.4:4] *the enemy*,[Mat.13:39] *the tempter*,[Mat.4:3] *the wicked one*,[Mat.13:19] *the ruler of darkness*,[Eph.6:12] *the murderer*,[Jn.8:44] and by other names.

You will meet him in his most subtle form as *the accuser*.[Rev.12:10]

So when you are discouraged, or tempted to doubt your experience with God, rehearse these *fifty-two facts* of GOD'S LIFE IN YOU.

That is the effective way to *resist the devil*, and James said *he will flee from you*. [Jas.4:7]

The apostle John said, *They overcame Satan by the word of their testimony;*[Rev.12:11] and Jesus defeated every temptation of Satan by saying, *It is written,*[Mat.4:4,7,10] then by quoting a scripture.

When the accuser tempts you, rehearse these facts and confess these scriptures and it will happen to you as it did to Jesus: *Then the devil left him, and, behold, angels came and ministered to him.*[Mat.4:11]

So, learn these facts on the next pages, and make these verses your confession.

Chapter 2

–52 Facts–
Of God's Life in You

1 **You were unsaved before you received Christ.**

For all have sinned, and come short of the glory of God.^{Rom.3:23}

2 **You were guilty before God, under the penalty of death.**

For the wages of sin is death.^{Rom.6:23}

3 **But God loved you too much to see you perish.**

He is not willing that any should perish, but that all should come to repentance.^{2Pet.3:9}

4 **God offered His best to prove His love to you.**

God so loved the world that he gave his only begotten Son, that whoever believes in him shall not perish, but have everlasting life.[Jn.3:16]

5 **Christ was God's gift and He died for you.**

But God commends his love toward us, in that while we were yet sinners, Christ died for us.[Rom.5:8]

6 **You realize that your sins separated you from God.**

Your iniquities have separated between you and your God, and your sins have hid his face from you.[Isa.59:2]

7 **Knowing your sins cost God His Son, and Jesus His life and blood, you repent of them.**

You sorrowed to repentance; for godly sor-

row works toward repentance [2Cor.7:9-10] and you know that *except you repent, you shall perish.*[Lu.13:3]

8 **You confess your sins to Him and are cleansed.**

If we confess our sins, he is faithful and just to forgive us our sins, and to cleanse us from all unrighteousness.[1Jn.1:9]

9 **You recognize Jesus at the door of your heart. You open it and He comes in.**

Behold, I stand at the door, and knock: if you hear my voice, and open the door, I will come in and will sup with you and you with me [Rev. 3:20] meaning to dine and have fellowship together.

10 **You receive Jesus and become God's child.**

As many as received Jesus Christ, to them

he gave power to become the children of God, even to them that believe on his name.[Jn.1:12]

11 You become a new creature.

If any one be in Christ that one is a new creature: old things are passed away; behold, all things are become new.[2Cor.5:17]

12 You know you are born again because you receive Christ.

Jesus said, *You must be born again* [Jn.3:7] *and when you received Christ with power to become God's child,*[Jn.1:12] you were *born, not of blood, nor of the will of the flesh, nor of the will of a human being, but of God,*[Jn.1:.13] *by the word of God which lives forever.*[1Pet.1:23]

13 You believe the powerful message of The Gospel that saves you.

The gospel is the power of God to salvation to every one that believes.[Rom.1:16]

14 **You believe on the name of Jesus Christ because of the record of the Gospels.**

These are written, that you might believe that Jesus is the Christ, the Son of God; and that believing you might have life through his name. Jn.20:31

15 **You call on His name and are saved.**

Whoever shall call upon the name of the Lord shall be saved. Rom.10:13

16 **You recognize that Jesus is the only way to God.**

I am the way, the truth and the life: no one comes to the Father but by me Jn.14:6 *for there is one God, and one mediator between God and people, the man Christ Jesus.* 1Tim.2:5

17 **You know there is salvation in none other.**

Neither is there salvation in any other: for there is none other name under heaven given among men, whereby we must be saved.[Ac.4:12]

18 **You put your faith in Jesus as Savior.**

For by grace are you saved through faith; and that not of yourselves: it is the gift of God: not of works, lest any one should boast.[Eph. 2:8-9]

19 **You believe that the Lord comes into your life.**

I will dwell in them, and walk in them; and I will be their God, and they shall be my people. I will be a Father to you, and you shall be my sons and daughters, says the Lord Almighty.[2Cor.6:16,18]

20 **You do not trust in any good works or self-righteousness to be saved.**

Our righteousnesses are like filthy rags.[Isa. 64:6] Our salvation was *not of works, lest any one should boast.*[Eph.2:9]

21 **You are saved only by God's mercy.**

Not by works of righteousness which we have done, but according to his mercy he saved us, by the washing of regeneration, and renewing of the Holy Ghost; Which he shed on us abundantly through Jesus Christ our Savior; That being justified by his grace, we should be made heirs according to the hope of eternal life.[Tit.3:5-7]

22 **You know Christ's death justifies you before God.**

Being justified by faith, we have peace with God through our Lord Jesus Christ.[Rom.5:1]

23 **You know His blood remits your sins forever.**

This is my blood which is shed for many for

the remission of sins.^{Mat.26:28} *Being justified by his blood, we shall be saved from wrath through him.*^{Rom.5:9}

24 **You know you are cleansed from sin.**

To him that loved us, and washed us from our sins in his own blood; ^{Rev.1:5} *In whom we have redemption through his blood, even the forgiveness of sins.*^{Col.1:14}

25 **You know your sins are put away and forgotten.**

Behold the Lamb of God, which takes away the sin of the world, ^{Jn.1:29} *having removed our transgressions from us as far as the east is from the west* ^{Psa.103:12} *so that your sins and iniquities will he remember no more.*^{Heb.10:17}

26 **You know your sins were paid for by Christ's death.**

Who his own self bore our sins in his own body on the tree, that we, being dead to sins, should live to righteousness.[1Pet.2:24] *He was wounded for our transgressions. He was bruised for our iniquities: the chastisement of our peace was upon him.*[Isa.53:5]

27 **With your sins punished and washed away you know they can never condemn you again.**

There is therefore now no condemnation to them which are in Christ Jesus,[Rom.8:1] *for God made him who knew no sin, to be sin for us; that we might be made the righteousness of God in Christ* [2Cor.5:21] and *where remission is, there is no more offering for sin* [Heb.10:18] so that now nothing *shall separate us from the love of Christ.*[Rom. 8:35]

28 **You know when you accept Christ you receive His life.**

Those that have the Son have life,[1Jn.5:12] *for they that hear my word, and believe on him that sent me, have everlasting life, and shall not come into condemnation, but you are passed from death to life.*[Jn.5:24] *And this is life eternal, that they might know you the only true God, and Jesus Christ whom you have sent.*[Jn.17:3]

29 You know Satan will accuse you.

He is the accuser which accused them before our God day and night [Rev.12:10] just like he did to Job. [Job1:6-12]

30 You are not ignorant of His works.

Lest Satan should get an advantage of us: for we are not ignorant of his devices.[2Cor.2:11] For we know that he *comes to steal, and to kill, and to destroy.*[Jn.10:10]

31 You know how Jesus overcame him.

But he answered and said, it is written. [Mat.:4,7,10] *Then the devil left him, and, behold, angels came and ministered to him.*[Mat.4:11]

32 You know Jesus proved that Satan could not win.

Christ was in all points tempted like we are, yet without sin. Let us therefore come boldly to the throne of grace, that we may obtain mercy, and find grace to help in time of need. Heb.4:15-16

33 You know He faithfully helps you in temptation.

There is no temptation taken you but such as is common to humankind: but God is faithful, who will not suffer you to be tempted above that you are able; but will with the temptation also make a way to escape, that you may be able to bear it. 1Cor.10:13

34 You know that there are two weapons Satan can never resist.

And they overcame him...the devil who accused them before God day and night...

1) by the blood of the Lamb, and

2) *by the word of their testimony.*[Rev.12:10-11]

35 **You know Satan cannot win over your faith.**

Be sober, be vigilant; because your adversary the devil, as a roaring lion, walks about, seeking whom he may devour: Whom resist steadfast in the faith.[1Pet.5:8-9] *Resist the devil, and he will flee from you. Draw near to God, and he will draw near to you;*[Jas.4:7-8] *you who are the begotten of God keep yourself, and that wicked one touches you not.*[1Jn.5:18]

36 **You know your faith is the victory.**

For whoever is born of God overcomes the world: and this is the victory that overcomes the world, even our faith.[1Jn.5:4]

37 **You know not to love the world but to do God's will.**

Love not the world, neither the things that are in the world. If any one love the world, the love of the Father is not in them. For all that is in the world, the lust of the flesh, and the lust of the eyes, and the pride of life, is not of the Father, but is of the world. And the world passes away, and the lust thereof; but those who do the will of God live for ever.[1Jn.2:15-17]

38 You know Christ came to defeat your enemy.

For this purpose the Son of God was manifested, that he might destroy the works of the devil.[1Jn.3:8]

39 You know Satan is no match for Christ in you.

Christ in you, the hope of glory.[Col.1:27] *I will dwell in you and walk in you, says the Lord Almighty.*[2Cor.6:16,18] *You are of God, little children and have overcome, because greater is he that is in you than he that is in the world.*[1Jn.4:4]

40 You know your new life source is the Lord Jesus Christ.

*I am crucified with Christ: nevertheless I live; yet not I, but Christ lives in me: and the life which I now live in the flesh I live by the faith of the Son of God, who loved me, and gave himself for me.*Gal.2:20

41 You know your new life has divine purpose.

*The steps of good people are ordered by the Lord and God delights in their way. Though they fall, they shall not be utterly cast down: for the Lord upholds them with his hand.*Psa. 37:23-24

42 You know God sees you and hears you.

For the eyes of the Lord are over the righteous and his ears are open to their prayers. 1Pet.3:12

43 You know He invites you to call on Him.

*Call to me, and I will answer you.*Jer.33:3

Ask, and it shall be given you; seek, and you shall find; knock, and it shall be opened to you. For every one that asks receives.^{Lu.11:9-10}

44 **You know when you pray that He answers.**

Whatever you desire, when you pray, believe that you receive them, and you shall have them; ^{Mk.11:24} *and whatever you shall ask in my name, that will I do, that the Father may be glorified in the Son.* ^{Jn.14:13}

45 **You know that you belong to God's royal family.**

You are a chosen generation, a royal priest-hood, an holy nation, a peculiar people; that you should show forth the praises of him who has called you out of darkness into his marvelous light.^{1Pet.2:9}

46 **You know that all Christ has now belongs to you.**

For all who are led by the spirit of God are

children of God. And so we should not be like cringing, fearful slaves, but we should behave like God's very own children, adopted into the bosom of his family, and calling him, "Father, Father" For his Holy Spirit speaks to us deep in our hearts, and tells us that we really are God's children. And since we are his children, we will share his treasures — for all God gives to his Son Jesus is now ours too.[Rom.8:14-17 LB]

47   You know you have His life in your flesh now.

That the life of Jesus might be made manifest in our mortal flesh,[2Cor.4:11] *for your body is the temple of the Holy Ghost.*[1Cor.6:19; 3:16-17]

48   You know you never need to live in want again.

My God shall supply all your need according to his riches in glory by Christ Jesus,[Phil. 4:19] *for no good thing will he withhold from them that walk uprightly.*[Psa.84:11]

49 You no longer fear diseases and plagues.

*There shall no evil befall you, neither shall any plague come near your dwelling,*Psa.91:10 *because I am the Lord who heals you.*Ex.15:26 *Jesus took our infirmities and bore our sicknesses* Mat.8:17 *and with his stripes we are healed.*Isa.53:5; 1Pet.2:24

50 You no longer are oppressed by problems.

*Casting all your care upon him; for he cares for you.*1Pet.5:7

51 You know you are a winner.

If God be for us, who can be against us? Rom.8:31 *...in all things we are more than conquerors through him that loved us.*Rom.8:37 *He which has begun a good work in you will perform it until the day of Jesus Christ.* Phil.1:6 *Faithful is he that calls you, who also will do it.*1Th.5:24

52 **You know Christ is with you to the end.**

*For he has said, I will never leave you, nor forsake you. So that we may boldly say, The Lord is my helper, and I will not fear what any person shall do to me,*Heb.13:5-6 *and, lo, I am with you alway, even to the end of the world.*Mat.28:20

THOSE 52 FACTS are for every man, woman, boy and girl who wants to fulfill God's dream for his or her life. They will foster in you a fresh discovery for experiencing a new kind of Divine Life and produce a *new hope, new faith, new love* and a *new purpose* in your life.

Chapter 3

—Greatest Miracle—
Of Your Life

IF YOU WILL only believe that Jesus suffered for you personally, you will be saved. Since your sins are *purged*,[Heb.1:3] they can no longer condemn you. The Lord wants to come and live in you; and when that happens, you are transformed by GOD'S LIFE IN YOU.

Right now, find a place alone with God, get on your knees and pray to the Lord right out loud. If you have accepted Christ, read the prayer that follows as a fresh confession of your faith and trust in Him.

If you have not yet embraced Jesus as a living reality in your life, do it now as you PRAY THIS PRAYER:

O Lord in heaven:

I do, here and now, believe on Jesus Christ, the Son of God. I believe that in Your great mercy and love, You died for me, as my personal substitute.

I believe that You suffered all of the penalty of my sins and that You paid the full price so that there is no more sin laid to my charge.

What love You manifested toward me, O Lord.

You were perfectly innocent. I was the guilty one. I had broken God's law. I should have been crucified. But You loved me too much to let me die for my own

sins. How I thank You for taking my place and for paying my full debt.

When You suffered my penalty, I was freed. There remain no sins to condemn me, so there is now no reason for me to be guilty before God. I can never be judged or sentenced for the sins which You died for. They were judged in You, Lord. All of my sins and old nature were put on Your account and You paid it all for me.

Now all of Your spotless righteousness is put to my account, so that I am now redeemed and saved.

Lord, I believe on Jesus Christ.

I do, here and now, welcome You into my heart as my Savior from sin, from hell, and from all the power of the devil.

I accept You, Jesus, as Lord of my life. I have come to You with all my heart, as a helpless, guilty sinner, seeking salvation, and trusting only in Your blood.

I trust that the blood of Jesus Christ blots out every sin and transgression from my life.

I trust that I am saved, by calling on the name of the Lord.

So from this day, I trust in what You did for me at the cross. It is enough. I am saved because of what You did for me. Nothing can ever improve my salvation.

I am now saved.

Thank You, Lord, for my full salvation.

I am redeemed. My sins are forgiven. I am saved. I believe on Jesus Christ. I trust in all You have done for me. It is enough. I am at peace. I am free from guilt and condemnation. I am a Christian—a follower of Jesus Christ, the Son of God.

Praise the Lord. Jesus saves me now.

From this moment, I shall strive to follow You and to share the Good News with others so that they can receive Your life too.

Amen.

If you believe the Bible promises contained in this book and if you have sincerely prayed and received Jesus into your life by faith, then your sins are forgiven.^{Col.1:14} An angel is recording your name *in the Lamb's book of life*,^{Rev.21:27} right now. Only believe. Jesus lives in you now. ^{Gal.2:20} You have His life.^{1Jn.5:12}

Registering your decision will be a lasting testimony of your personal experience today. If your enemy, the devil, ever tries to make you doubt what has taken place, you will refer to the decision you recorded this day, and know that you have received the abundant life of Jesus Christ and have been born again.

As an act of faith, register your decision on the next page. Be definite about it. Receiving Christ as your Savior is the greatest miracle of your life.

MY DECISION

Today I have read this book, GOD'S LIFE IN YOU. I have sincerely and reverently prayed the prayer that is written here.

I believe I have received Jesus Christ in my own life and that I am reborn with His life. I commit my life to do my best to please Him in all that I think and say and do. With His grace and help, I shall share Jesus Christ with others.

Relying on Him to keep me by His grace, I have made this decision today— in Jesus' name.

Signature: _____

Date: _____

A new miracle life has begun for you. Our greatest reward is to receive testimonies from those who have been reborn as a result. I would be very pleased if you would let us know and tell us that you have accepted Jesus Christ, and that you have received the miracle of the new birth.

From the day your testimony reaches us, we will be earnestly praying for God's best to come to you and your loved ones. Stay in touch with us and we will help you in your new walk with Christ. There are many ministry resources available on our Osborn.org website to help you grow in your faith and to help you experience all that Christ has made available to you. Your decision to follow Christ is the *beginning* of your new life of purpose with Him.

We pray for every person who reads this book. You and we are now partners in following and serving Jesus Christ.

T. L. Osborn

T.L. and Daisy Osborn were teammates in evangelism for over half a century, proclaiming the gospel of Christ and sharing His love with millions of people, face to face, in more than 70 nations. Here they rejoice together on the final day of another triumphant soulwinning crusade.

OSBORN CRUSADES WORLDWIDE. For over six decades, in over 100 nations, The Osborn family has been a pace-setter in mass-evangelism. It is believed Drs. T.L. & Daisy have shared Christ with more non-Christians, face to face, than any couple who has ever lived.

CARIBBEAN – Ponce, Puerto Rico

AFRICA – Kinshasa, Zaire

INDONESIA – Surabaya, Java

MEXICO – Monterrey

PHILIPPINES – Cabanatuan

T.L. and Daisy Osborn
Mass Miracle
Evangelism
Crusades

HONDURAS – Tegucigalpa

JAPAN – Kyoto

EAST AFRICA – Mombasa, Kenya

PHILIPPINES – Davao, Mindanao

S. AMERICA – Bogota, Colombia

This lad is hoisted above the shoulders of those who saw him take his first miracle steps following T.L.'s message and mass prayer for healing. He is brought through the crowd, to the platform in Nakuru, where all can see the wonder of his miracle.

INSET: As the multitude looked with amazement, the young man, with the steel brace and shoes lifted high, marched across the platform to show the miracle God had done for him.

OSBORN MINISTRIES –

- Angola
- Argentina
- Armenia
- Australia
- Austria
- Azerbaijan
- Bangladesh
- Belarus
- Belgium
- Benin
- Bermuda
- Bolivia
- Botswana
- Brazil
- Bulgaria
- Burkina Faso
- Burundi

- Cambodia
- Cameroon
- Canada
- Central Afr. Rep.
- Chad
- Chile
- China
- Colombia
- Congo (Dem. Rep.)
- Congo (Rep.)
- Costa Rica
- Cuba
- Denmark
- Dominican Rep.
- Ecuador
- Egypt
- El Salvador
- England
- Estonia
- Ethiopia
- Finland
- France
- Gabon

- Georgia
- Germany
- Ghana
- Guatemala
- Haiti
- Honduras

LEGEND

Nations in which the Osborns have proclaimed the Gospel in face-to-face ministry.

And he said unto them, Go ye into all the worl[d]

OVER 60 YEARS – OVER 100 NATIONS

- Hong Kong
- India
- Indonesia
- Ireland
- Italy
- Ivory Coast
- Jamaica
- Japan
- Kazakhstan
- Kenya
- Kyrgyzstan
- Laos
- Liberia
- Lithuania
- Luxemborg
- Madagascar
- Malawi
- Malaysia
- Mexico
- Mongolia
- Myanmar
- Netherlands

- New Zealand
- Nicaragua
- Nigeria
- Norway
- Pakistan
- Panama
- Papua N.Guinea
- Paraguay
- Peru
- Philippines
- Poland
- Portugal
- Puerto Rico
- Russia

- Rwanda
- Senegal
- South Africa
- South Korea
- Spain
- Sri Lanka
- Sweden
- Switzerland
- Taiwan
- Tajikistan
- Tanzania
- Thailand
- Togo
- Trinidad
- Uganda
- Ukraine
- United States
- Uruguay
- Uzbekistan
- Venezuela
- Vietnam
- Virgin Islands
- Zambia

nd preach the gospel to every creature.^{Mk.16:15}

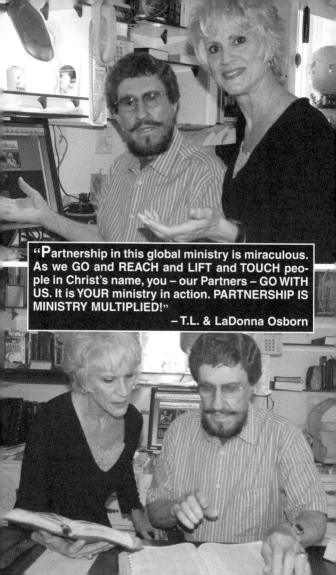

"**P**artnership in this global ministry is miraculous. As we GO and REACH and LIFT and TOUCH people in Christ's name, you – our Partners – GO WITH US. It is YOUR ministry in action. PARTNERSHIP IS MINISTRY MULTIPLIED!"

– T.L. & LaDonna Osborn

"**We** have one message – Christ and His ministry to forgive, heal and restore people to fellowship with God. Every person is included in God's great love-plan. This is the GOOD NEWS that Christ wants told!"
– T.L. & LaDonna Osborn

T.L. & LaDonna Osborn Miracle Crusade–Medellin, Colombia

LaDonna C. Osborn

T.L. & LaDonna Osborn Miracle-Life Conference– Amlaty, Kyrghyzstan, an ex-Soviet Republic. 10 Osborn books in Russian are given to every adult.

T.L. & Daisy Osborn Mass Miracle Crusade – Bogota, S. America

Thousands attend the T.L. & LaDonna Osborn *Miracle-Life* Conference in this ancient Muslim nation of Kyrghyzstan–bordering West China.

T.L. Osborn

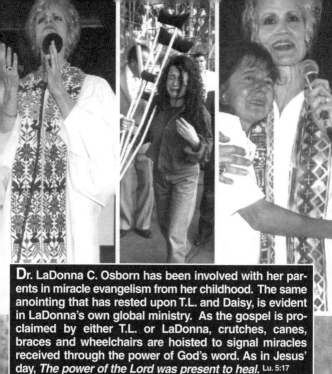

Dr. LaDonna C. Osborn has been involved with her parents in miracle evangelism from her childhood. The same anointing that has rested upon T.L. and Daisy, is evident in LaDonna's own global ministry. As the gospel is proclaimed by either T.L. or LaDonna, crutches, canes, braces and wheelchairs are hoisted to signal miracles received through the power of God's word. As in Jesus' day, *The power of the Lord was present to heal.* Lu. 5:17

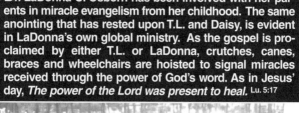

Preacher

Teacher

Leader

Dr. LaDonna C. Osborn's life and ministry are focused on reaching the UNreached, then on building each convert into a reproductive member of the Body of Christ.

As Bishop of more than 700 churches, her passion is to see that each soul won to Christ becomes part of a local church where they learn to function as His representative in sharing His love with others.

Her dynamic courses on Redemption are preferred by leaders worldwide, to ground believers in the Bible truths of Christ's work.

Just as in Bible days, Dr. LaDonna goes and preaches everywhere, the Lord working with her and confirming the word through the accompanying signs. (Mk 16:20 paraphrased)

The cripples are walking. The blind are seeing. The deaf are hearing. Cancers are disappearing. Hundreds of physical healing miracles are confirming the message of God's love and saving plan for people.

The ministries of the Osborns have made an unprecedented impact on the world. They are considered by church leaders worldwide to be among the great soulwinners of our epoch. Dr. T.L. Osborn, Dr. Daisy Washburn-Osborn (1924-1995) and Dr. LaDonna C. Osborn have ministered in over 100 nations.

The *MISSION*
Of Christianity

THE GLOBAL MISSION of Christianity is to witness of Christ and of His resurrection to *the entire world—* to *every creature.*Mk.16:15

The Apostle Paul said, *Whoever shall call on the name of the Lord shall be saved.*Rom.10:13

T.L. and Daisy Osborn shared a worldwide ministry together for over five decades, before her demise in 1995. T.L. resolved to continue his global ministry to multitudes.

The Osborn daughter, Dr. LaDonna, assumed a prominent role in the leadership of the Osborns' world ministry. As the fame of her preaching ministry spread, she continued being involved in public mass evangelism *Festivals of Faith and Miracles* and/or trans-evangelical *Gospel Seminars* in fields of the world such as *Indonesia*, nations of *French-speaking Africa, South America, Eurasia* and the world's most populous nation, *China.*

As CEO of *OSBORN Ministries International*, Dr. LaDonna's expertise is making possible the expansion of this ministry in nations around the world. Learn more about the Osborn Global Outreaches through their website at ***osborn.org.***

Drs. T.L., Daisy and LaDonna Osborn have reached millions for Christ in over a hundred nations during more than six decades. This ministry-brief is included here to inspire young believers that they, too, can carry the *gospel torch into all the world.*Mk.16:15

Mass Miracle Evangelism

Tommy Lee Osborn and Daisy Marie Washburn were married in Los Banos, California in 1942, at the ages of 17 and 18. In 1945 they went to India as missionaries but were unable to convince the people of these ancient religions—Muslims and Hindus—about Christ. They had not yet discovered the truths about healing miracles. They returned to the USA dismayed and disheartened—but not dissuaded.

Soon after their demoralizing return home, the Lord appeared to them both, at different times, as they searched for the answer to their dilemma.

- They began to discover the Bible truths that create faith for biblical miracles.

- They had learned in India that for people of non-Christian nations to believe the gospel, they must witness miracle proof that Jesus Christ is alive today.

- They discovered that signs, miracles and wonders are essential to convincing *non*-Christian nations about the gospel.

> *Jesus* was…*approved of God among people by **miracles** and **wonders** and **signs**, which God did by Him in the midst of the people.*^{Ac.2:22}

These dynamic truths created in their spirits fresh faith in God's Word. With this new lease on life and having discovered the scriptural facts about miracles they, along with their children, *re*-launched their soulwinning saga in 1949—this time in the Caribbean island-nation of Jamaica.

During thirteen weeks of ministry there,

hundreds of biblical miracles confirmed their preaching.

- Over a hundred deaf-mutes were healed;

- Over ninety totally blind people received sight;

- Hundreds of crippled, paralyzed and lame people were restored;

- Most important of all, *nearly ten thousand souls received Jesus Christ as their Savior.*

That success motivated their new global ministry, proclaiming the gospel to multitudes. In the era when developing nations were mostly *colonized* by European governments, the Osborns pioneered the concept of *Mass Miracle Evangelism.* Such methods had not been witnessed since the epoch of the Early Church. T.L. and Daisy addressed audiences of tens of thousands throughout the dangerous years of *nationalism* when the awakening of many developing nations was repulsing foreign political domination.

Their example inspired national men and women, globally, to arise from their restrictive past, and to become leading gospel messengers and church builders in the unevangelized nations of the world. Many of them are numbered among the most distinguished and successful Christian leaders today.

The largest churches in the world are no longer in America or Europe. Anointed and talented national pastors are raising them up. Single churches in Africa seat 50,000 plus people. To God be the glory.

Drs. T.L. and Daisy's partial testimony is recorded for posterity in their 512 page unique pictorial, THE GOSPEL ACCORDING TO T.L. AND DAISY.

Global Evangelism Concepts

During T.L. and Daisy's unprecedented years as an evangelism team, they inaugurated numerous programs to reach the unreached. Their concept of *National Missionary Assistance* resulted in them sponsoring over 30,000 national preachers as full time missionaries to unevangelized tribes and villages where new, self-supporting churches became established globally.

The Osborn literature is published in more than 130 languages. Their Docu-Miracle crusade films, audio and video CDs and DVDs, and their digital productions (including Bible courses), are produced in over 70 languages and are circulated around the world.

They have provided airlifts and huge shipments of literature and of soulwinning tools for gospel ministries abroad.

They have furnished scores of four-wheel drive vehicles equipped with films, projectors, screens, generators, public-address systems, audiocassettes and cassette players, plus literature for reaching the unreached.

Publishing The Gospel

Dr. Daisy's five major books are *pace-setters* in Christian literature for women — *unique examples of **inclusive** language that consistently addresses both men and women.*

Dr. T.L. has authored over 20 major books. He wrote his first, HEALING THE SICK, during their mission to Jamaica in 1950. Now in its 46th edition, it is a global favorite, used as a Bible School text book in many nations.

The publisher calls HEALING THE SICK — *A Living Classic* — a faith-building best seller since 1950. Over a million copies are in print, circulating healing truth throughout the world.

Dr. LaDonna's book, GOD'S BIG PICTURE is published in scores of languages and is heralded globally as the single most important book to make clear the story of the Bible, from Genesis to Revelation. Through this book, people discover their place in God's plan.

Some of her other books, such as CHAOS OF MIRACLES and UNKNOWN BUT NOT FORGOTTEN are modern day accounts of Christ's ministry in action through her today as she ministers the gospel among some of the world's unreached masses.

Their Global Saga

In T.L.'s ninth decade of life, the Osborn Ministries International continues to expand. Following Daisy's demise, T.L.

has continued his global evangelism crusades, and his daughter, Dr. LaDonna,
has enlarged her ministries of evangelism
and training to nearly every continent as
she carries the *torch of the gospel* into this
century's new frontiers.

Like the Apostle Paul, LaDonna says:

> *I am not ashamed of the gospel of Christ,
> for it is the power of God to salvation
> to everyone who believes.* Rom.1:16

She believes that:

*The World is the **Heart** of the Church,*
*The Church is the **Hope** of the World.*

She contends that:

Without the *World*, the *Church* is **meaningless**—
Without the *Church*, the *World* is **hopeless**.

Colonialism
Nationalism
Globalism/Evangelism

Dr. LaDonna Osborn knows the ministry of World Evangelism. Since childhood, she has lived on the front lines of global SOULWINNING — from the days of *colonialism,* through the turbulent years of *nationalism,* and into this century of *globalism, mass evangelism* and *national* and *international Church growth.*

The Osborns hold forth these simple truths:

1) That the Bible is as valid today as it ever was;

2) That the divine calling for every believer is to witness of Christ to the unconverted;

3) That every soul won to Christ can become His representative; and

GOD'S LIFE IN YOU

4) That miracles, signs and wonders are what distinguish Christianity from being just another philosophical religion.

To demonstrate these biblical issues is the essence of the global *MISSION of Christianity.*

Just as with the Apostle Paul, Dr. LaDonna and Dr. T.L. state:

> *The ministry we have received of the Lord is to testify to the gospel of the grace of God;* Ac.20:24 *to preach the gospel in the regions beyond.*2Cor.10:16

The history of the Osborn Ministries International is also recorded in their unique and historical 24-volume *Encyclo-Biographical Anthology.* It contains more than 23,000 pages, 30,946 photos, 636 *Faith Digest* magazines, 2,024 pages of personal, hand-written diary notes, 1,011 pages of Osborns' news letters, 1,062 pages of unpublished historical data about their world ministry, 2,516 world mission reports, and 6,113 Christian ministry reports.

These 24 giant tomes span over six feet of shelf space and have taken their place in the archives and libraries of institutions of higher learning around the world, including such renowned universities and libraries as: University of Cambridge, Cambridge, England; University of Oxford, Oxford, England; Asbury Theological Seminary, Wilmore, USA; British Library, London, England; Central Bible College, Springfield, USA; Christ for the Nations, Dallas, USA; Fuller Theological Seminary, Pasadena, USA; Messenger College, Joplin, USA; National Library, Sofia, Bulgaria; ORU, Tulsa, USA; Ramkhamhaeng University, Bangkok, Thailand; Regent University, Virginia Beach, USA; Universidad Interamericana de Puerto Rico, Ponce, Puerto Rico; Université de Cocody,

Abidjan, Ivory Coast; University of Ghana, Legon-Accra, Ghana; Université de Kinshasa, Kinshasa, Democratic Republic of the Congo; Université de Lomé, Lomé, Togo; University of Nairobi, Nairobi, Kenya; University of Maseno, Maseno, Kenya; Université Marien Ngouabi, Brazzaville, Congo; Université Omar Bongo, Libreville, Gabon; University of Wales, Bangor, Wales; Vernadsky National Library, Kiev, Ukraine; Word of Life, Uppsala, Sweden; (plus many more), and the archives of many leading denominational headquarters.